Tam's Stories

An Israeli Woman Lawyer in America

Tamar Frankel

ISBN 978-1-888215-87-8

Printed in the United States
Fathom Publishing Company
PO Box 200448, Anchorage, AK 99520-0448
https://tamarfrankel.com
https://fathompublishing.com

To my husband Raymond Atkins
and my children Anat Bird and Michael Frankel

—Tamar Frankel

Contents

Introduction

As one advances in age, especially when one crosses the 80 line, children, friends and colleagues ask for a story of one's life. The pressure becomes especially acute for those who happened to be a "first" of something, like a first woman professor at a particular American law school (though not the first woman professor at any law school). I never wanted to look backwards and always had something far more interesting and challenging looking forward. Besides, the past does not let go anyway. It interferes with what one does whether one wants it or not. Sometimes I say or do something only to realize where it came from, long ago. So, I felt that the past locked me into the present and marked my future anyway. Why focus on it even more?

Then, one day, I was listening to one of Alexander McCall Smith's many books. I listened to books on tape when driving to work, a trip of about 45 minutes. These must be books that are not too deep to distract me completely from driving and lead to an accident, but not too uninteresting as to lose their value in making the frequent trip more tolerable. Reflecting on Master Smith's stories, and he is indeed a master, it occurred to me that I could tell the story of my life by focusing on what is far more important than myself. That is, focusing on the people with whom I interacted, the ideas that I have heard and generated, the issues that an immigrant faces, and above all, the society in which I lived. A story of this sort might reproduce a "chunk" of life.

I stopped to consider an important aspect of Smith's work—his humor—and wondered whether I could follow in his footsteps. Without this aspect, the value of reading my story would diminish and perhaps disappear. Smith has wonderful humor. Not a biting cynical humor, but loving, understanding, and, sometimes appreciative, humor. I am not sure to what extent, if at all, I could tell a story this way.

Out of the fog of memories came the moment in which my mother sat in an easy chair in our apartment's veranda in Tel Aviv. The easy chair was like those you see at the sea shore. Its back and base were made of rough cloth. I must have been eight or ten, standing near my mother, when the cloth began to tear. It must have been torn already at one side of the chair, and we were hearing the crunchy sound of tearing. Before Mother could say or do anything, the cloth tore completely. Mother's bottom hit the floor and her legs were pointing straight up. She was encased in the wooden frame of the chair, unable to lift herself. Both of us were frozen for a moment. Then mother said, quite loudly: "Tamar, help me up!"

Instead of giving her a helping hand, I felt a tickle in my throat that quickly rose and became a roaring laughter. I stood there, helplessly laughing. Only when laughter subsided could I hold out a hand to my mother and help pull her up. At that point, both of us just broke out into laughter. We did not chuckle. We did not laugh hysterically. We laughed uncontrollably. Laughter took over. We could not stop, until we finally did.

Is this story humorous? If it is not humor, what is it? I loved my mother deeply. She was caught in that chair. There was nothing funny in her situation. And yet, it was funny, and after she was freed from the chair, she recognized the "funniness" as well. It may have been funny because of her posture or the surprise, and it may have been funny to see her helplessness and recognize the reversed position we suddenly faced when I was the one to help her. What was truly wonderful was the fact that she laughed as well. She understood and joined me, and she laughed at herself. That she could do so is one reason why I loved her so much. This incident helped me understand that, although I cannot possibly match Smith's humor, I could follow his brand of humor, telling the story and understanding why we laugh.

The hardest issue in preparing this story was choosing the narrator. Should I speak in the first person, "I language?" Would it not be better and more comfortable to speak in the "she language" and distance myself from the narrator in order to tell the story more objectively? "I" was far too close. There is also a selfish aura in "I." As if the narrator rather than the story is the focus. "She language" is therefore better. But "she" had to have a name. An artificial name was too distant. An entirely different name would require another character. Yet, in the story of my life, I, not someone else, am the character. The solution was to give "she" a name that was close to mine but not completely mine. And the shorter the better: "Tam."

Chapter One
Coming to America

Walking on the banks of the Charles River in Boston was an exhilarating experience. When Tam came to America in 1963, as a visiting scholar at Harvard Law School, she walked many hours on the bank of the river. For the first time in her life, and she was about 38 then, she was anonymous. She was free in a new way. She had full privacy. In her native Israel, privacy was not possible and hardly valued. One could walk in the street, and a woman might approach, touch the cloth of one's blouse, and ask: "Hey, where did you get these fabrics?" Or one could come home from work and meet one's neighbor, Dushinka, who would ask: "Do you eat chocolate pudding often?" Dushinka has been to Tam's kitchen and opened and peered into her fridge. Or one could walk with one's child age three in the pram, as Tam walked one day. It was a very hot day, and she bought her son ice cream in a cone. He licked with relish as the melting ice cream was running down his chin onto his little shirt. So Tam took the shirt off, and the ice cream glistened in her son's happy face and on his chest. As she passed a taxi stand, one of the drivers pointed his finger at her accusingly. "What are you doing?" he said. "The child must have a shirt on. Otherwise, he will catch a cold!" That was Israel.

On the other hand, she thought, "I should not be quick to judge these intrusions." If I walked in Tel Aviv at two o'clock at night, alone, and shouted: "Help!" A 100 people will fill the street in a moment to ask what is wrong. When Tam visited New York, she found that it was reported and widely believed that no one called the police, even when people watched a woman being murdered in front of their buildings. Many years later, it was reported that there were calls to the police and other efforts to help the woman, but the failure to help remains better known and believed.[*]

In New York, people did not want to get involved. In Tel Aviv, they wanted to get involved. So the reason is not that people were good or bad, or valued privacy in one place more than in another. Perhaps the reason is the social feeling of security. Americans felt secure as a nation. No one had attacked their country for many years. Israel was tiny, compared to the size of America. It had many enemies and was under attack most, if not all, of the time. To survive, the Israeli society and the country needed to sacrifice privacy and adopt the attitude of getting involved. That was the price of safety and security, and it was not such a high price to pay, even if the intruding taxi driver became loudly irritated. Later, Tam observed that with time Israel changed. Still later, Israel had an army, planes and modern military equipment. When Tam lived in Israel, there was a fairly small army, a small community, restructured Messerschmitt airplanes and little military equipment, modern or ancient. As time went by, Tam discovered the price of privacy, and that price was not as low as she initially believed.

---

[*]   https://www.newsweek.com/fact-check-did-38-witnesses-do-nothing-while-kitty-genovese-was-killed-1964-1579901

Chapter Two
Loss of Identity

Tam was having coffee at the LL.M. students' lounge at Harvard Law School. The group of students included both American born and foreigners from different parts of the world. They usually found their kind and clustered in small groups, some speaking their native language. Tam did not meet any Israeli students. She sat alone, drinking her coffee, when an American student joined her. "Where are you from?" he asked, and she told him. "Do you like it here?" He asked. "Oh, yes," she said, "Very much. And you?" She asked. He was from Nebraska. The conversation died soon, and they parted.

Tam realized all of a sudden that she had no identity at that time and place. For this American student, she was two-dimensional, just a face and nothing behind it of substance. Suddenly, she wanted to stand up and say: "I am Israeli born. My father was born in Czechoslovakia and my mother in Dubosar, Russia, near the large river Dnister. Father arrived in Israel in 1920, and Mother when she was two years old, in 1904 probably. Father was the first president of the Israeli Bar Association. When he arrived, he was one of five Jewish lawyers in Tel Aviv, or perhaps in the entire Jewish community."

In America, Tam wanted to build her third dimension. She felt empty. She wanted people to know who she was when they looked at her, without the need to tell them who she was, what she had done or not done, and who her family was. She did not want to see their blank look. Their eyes were sometimes interested. Tam was not only good looking; she could be beautiful and sometimes exude sexiness that both men and women who came

13

in touch with her felt. So the eyes looking at her were sometimes interested. But American eyes were often blank. They knew nothing about Tam. And whether they were interested to know, or whether Tam was interested in offering the information about her third dimension was a difficult issue.

Chapter Three
America Has an Identity As Well

Tam found that America had an identity that was blank to her. Although she knew English quite well, she did not know idioms and popular expressions. What did this person mean when saying: "I will take my marbles and go home?" The dictionary does not explain. After hearing the statement in a variety of contexts, one can figure it out. It means that I will not play anymore, I refuse to participate in this project and I will take any parts that are uniquely mine. America has many such expressions, so a foreigner can easily be overwhelmed by them.

Tam did not understand and was not interested in football, baseball, and hockey, let alone golf. Years later, when she taught corporate law, she reviewed a case that dealt with the NFL. She judged the results of the case and the court's analysis to be poor. So, she said to the class: "I am not particularly impressed by this case. In addition, I do not know anything about baseball." And the entire class howled with laughter. Baseball was not football, students explained, and NFL was the National Football League. So much for sports.

But there were other cultural blanks that were more pressing and harder to uncover. You cannot easily find out whether one should address practicing lawyers as Mr. So and So, or Harry and Joe. And how do you sign the letter addressed to them? Tam, or Dr. or Professor? And when the lawyers suggest a meeting at 12:00 does it mean that the three of you will go to lunch, or stay to work and eat no lunch together? One must ask someone. The right person to ask is the issue, and how many such questions can you ask?

Sometimes, one cannot even ask but should figure it out. In Israel, if you found that you left your wallet at home and needed five pounds, you knocked on a colleague's door and borrowed to repay tomorrow. Or you "bummed" a cigarette instead of running outside to buy a pack. But the cold eyes and slightly-lifted nose told Tam that this is not the way people behave in America, at least not in her environment and not in 1963.

On the other hand, in America, everyone asks everyone else: "How are you?" without waiting for an answer. Usually the answer is very short: "Fine, how are you?" To which the first inquirer says: "Fine, thanks." And both move on, having shared almost nothing. In Israel, if one asked: "How are you?" it was a question. The answer was then given in detail. If you did not want to hear a detailed answer, you did not ask the question. In America, "How are you" was the alternative to "Hi." You had to figure it out by yourself. The sooner the better. Or else you would be deemed rude if you failed to ask the question, and a bore if you answered in detail the Israeli way.

Chapter Four
Experiences When New at Boston University

When Tam was hired as a faculty member at Boston University Law School, she had advantages over many of her colleagues. She had an LL.M. and SJ.D. at Harvard Law School and had already written and published, more than most, if not all, of her colleagues. Yet, attached to being the only woman teacher, were the different images of the other faculty's wives and women generally. On top of that, being a Jew, being a woman with these Harvard recognitions, distinguished Tam as well.

There were assumptions regarding Tam's behavior which did not fit what the faculty usually experienced before and mainly

Boston University School of Law Faculty photo taken on April 17, 1969. Tamar Frankel, the School of Law's first female professor, is standing on the far right.
Photo by Boston University Photography.

after she was hired. Tam adjusted to some of their expectations, and the faculty adjusted to the fact that Tam would be what she is.

In sum, an adjustment to the addition of a very different person to the usual ranks may take time and require change by both parties. What was also helpful (perhaps) was a letter by a New York insurance regulator. He wrote to thank Tam for the study of Variable Annuities which could be followed by the insurance department. It provided that both parties move to accepting with moderate change the basic assumption and behavior of the other party.

Finally, the behavior of the Dean of the School (or division of the business) and the President of the University provided the basic approach and respect to the different newcomer. This approach gave the newcomer the greatest incentive to adjust to the culture of the University and school provided the adjustment does not basically conflict with the newcomer's fundamental values. This last condition applies to the newcomer into another organization. A joke about a Jew requires a response by a joke about the Christians that the Jews spawned and so on.

This conclusion is a repetition of the beginning. You may be different, but if you contribute, you are valuable to your institution. You do not give up an inch to the required respect that you justly deserve.

Chapter Five
Falling Between the Three Worlds

Before Tam decided to stay in America permanently, she had a serious talk with herself. No matter how intrusive Israelis were, members of the community were truly members. No matter how congested the small community felt. No matter how much one sometimes wanted to breathe air free of intrusion by government, bureaucrats, friends, acquaintances, and everyone you did not know but who knew you or your parents or family. No matter all these pressures—you belonged. You did not always belong to what or where you wanted to belong. But you belonged.

Tam had never experienced the lack of a sense of belonging. On the contrary! She could knock on the door of a Supreme Court Justice and just come in because she played piano in his home when she was a student in Jerusalem or because he was her boss and the Director of the Ministry of Justice when she worked there in 1949.

She had family connections going back to 1870 (with an uncle of her mother's), professional connections through her father and afterwards herself, friends or acquaintances during school years, in the underground and the Israeli Air Force. All these brought a deep sense of belonging and sometimes a sense of communal pressure.

Tam remembered with nostalgia her trip at the age of twelve or thirteen to Kibbutz Kfar Giladi during the Passover break. The son of her mother's uncle came to fetch her and take her with him. He was a gorgeous 17-year-old young man and she felt the tremor of more than friendship for him. He was charming and protective, and it was the first time she was going alone and far away. The Kibbutz is at the northern part of the country abutting Lebanon's border. The Seder in Passover was nothing she had ever experienced. There were hundreds of people: Members of the Kibbutz, their wives and children and friends and extended family, such as herself, from other places. It was a Seder not of a family but a community, and yet this community became an extended family.

Not all relationships were smooth. There were arguments about the organizers and the managers, some of whose children studied at the expense of the community (sometimes abroad). There were issues of burden of work and allocation of tasks. There were sympathies and lack of sympathies. These passions and disagreements among community members paralleled those among family members.

Tam did not note the depths of passion and disagreements within the members of the community when she came to visit. She saw the beautiful mountains, the communal singing and dancing. She had a wonderful time even though she also was somewhat jealous of an older distant cousin who wore "silk stockings" and attracted attention (justly—she was beautiful, Tam had to admit). Nonetheless, it was her family that built this Kibbutz. It was her mother's uncle who was the director of a large project to convert swamp land into habitable land (Mifal HaChula).

Talking to the young American lawyer at the LL.M. students' lounge at Harvard Law School, Tam was tempted to tell him all these facts, but could not. Somehow it did not seem natural to suddenly say: "Let me tell you who I am and who my family members were." What would this American student understand if she told him that her father, who came to Israel as a Zionist, having acquired a doctorate in law and in economics at the University of Vienna, wanted to work with his hands! Jews, her father believed should be like everyone else and only then could they build a State and cease to be persecuted. He applied at a construction firm to work as a builder. But after only two weeks, the foreman called him. "Dr. Hofmann," he said, "This will not work. Please go and practice law." Her father was crushed. But as everyone in the family knew, he had "two left hands." He could not be a construction worker. He had to practice law.

How could Tam tell the full story without describing the time and space in which these events occurred and the irony of a Zionist who wants the Jewish nation to be populated with workers "like everyone else" instead of a bunch of intellectuals?

In the United States, Tam fell between the Israeli and American Jewish communities. A year or so before she came to the United States, she had served as the legal adviser in the Israel Bonds organization in Europe. Most of her work was not law but promotion. Yet, to some extent the two were linked. In any event, one evening she was at a party in Switzerland. Everyone was telling funny stories, and she ventured to tell one. She said:

> During the First World War, Cohen served in the Infantry. When his platoon came to a bridge, Cohen was sent by the commander to see whether the Army (horses and cannons as well as infantry) could cross the bridge. Reporting to his commander, Cohen said: "The cannons can cross the bridge and the horses can cross the bridge. But the infantry cannot cross the bridge." "Why not?" asked the commander in surprise. "There are two large dogs at the end of the bridge," said Cohen.

Tam thought that the story was funny. But the listeners did not laugh. A silence descended on the group, and one of the members took her by the arm, moved her aside and said: "You should never tell this joke again. This is an anti-Semitic joke." It was indeed, for it made fun of Jews as people afraid of dogs, even Jews in the Army. Tam never knew an Israeli who was afraid of dogs, but the stereotype of a Jew included this feature. She was indeed telling an anti-Semitic joke. But it was also a joke she did not mind telling because, as an Israeli, she did not identify with such Jews.

The Israel that Tam left would be changed when she came back to Israel to visit. The America, where she settled, where she did not grow up or go to school and had no family connections and no social network, would always be somewhat foreign. The American Jewish community who viewed themselves differently from Israelis or at least the Israeli born was different. Tam felt that she did not belong fully to the American Jewish community either.

Tam knew about persecution by reading the history of the Jewish nation and understanding the reason Jews need a political State. In Israel, she never experienced anti-Semitism from those who were ruling the country. Tam and her friends ruled the country.

Chapter Six
About Choices and Risks

Tam was not a good lawyer by American standards. She had a very different education in a very different country. Her law school was the "Jerusalem Law Classes" housed in Jerusalem not far from the old city. It was the only school that qualified for the certificate authorizing "the practice of law" in Israel. The other avenue for practicing law during the British Mandate was to receive a barrister's status in England. That was not even considered in her family. So Jerusalem Law Classes was not a choice but the only choice.

Years later, when Tam spoke to a class of graduating students on their way to practice, she realized how lucky she was for having one choice. "When I came to America," she told the students, "I was brought to an ice cream store. There on the wall was the list of 33 flavors to choose from. Where I came from, there were just three: chocolate, vanilla and strawberry." I stood there thinking about a young person who was brought to the store for an ice cream cone and the anxiety that the person would experience in choosing among the 33 flavors. And, in addition, when I chose one flavor, I lost the chance to enjoy two flavors. When the young person in this store chose one flavor, he or she lost 32 flavors."

Then she added: "I can imagine the concern and anxiety of each of you, as you try and choose one job, one state, one specialization. But think of it! You are young. You do not have to specialize. You have not lost the opportunities to change and seek another job, another state and another specialization. It is only later that such decisions would close the door for you. Not yet. Not now." And Tam could almost hear a breath of relief. Not quite a sigh, but a letting of the air from the lungs.

The absence of choices helped Tam along the way. She was not raised with the richness of choice but neither was she raised with the anxiety of choices. Therefore, she was more willing to take a route and try it out without fear of losing other choices. They were there, waiting at least for a time, if she ever found that her initial choice was the wrong one. The choices did not produce a sense of dread of loss (making the wrong choice) but a sense of security (choices were the backup, in case this one did not work out). Tam concluded that more choices were better than fewer, provided the choices not taken are not viewed as permanent discards or losses but as backups to opportunities. They were doors that were left partly open if you did not choose to open them wide.

Because of her background and because of this approach, Tam took many risks in her work and learned from them. For example, when Tam first joined the faculty at her law school, she saw that the students were not organized as "clubs" to engage in what interested some of them, such as international business transactions. She knew about these clubs from observations at Harvard Law School, although when she wanted to join, she was politely discouraged. That happened because she did not know then that the clubs were populated, not by LL.M. students, but by LL.B. students (now J.D.).

So, after her first semester at her new school, she asked a number of students whether they would be interested in such a club and received an enthusiastic response from some of them. The students and Tam worked on a "constitution" and established the club, receiving support from the Dean, who viewed the initiative very positively and encouraged it.

The beginning of next year, however, Tam learned that another teacher, who taught public international law was to be the adviser to the club (that turned later into an international law review). She did ask the dean why she, who helped the students establish the club, was not appointed adviser. The Dean looked embarrassed, and after clearing his throat, suggested that Tam and the new appointee be co-advisers to the club. Tam was angry but not devastated. She thanked the Dean and told him that she would not co-advise. And that was that.

There were two other innovations that Tam had organized without faculty support. One was an interdisciplinary course together with two teachers of the University's Business School. It was a marvelous course. The students were so involved. They loved it, worked hard and learned a lot. The teachers found it an enormously time-consuming way of teaching that was exciting and interesting.

After the first year, Tam realized that neither the Business School nor her own Dean were going to support or even acknowledge the experiment. She and the two other teachers dropped the experiment. She did not dwell on the death of this experiment and did not even think much about it. But instinctively she chose another route. Almost 40! years later, she tried it again with the support of a Dean of another generation and at least some acknowledgment of another generation of colleagues. She was no genius, although she was able. She was simply a risk taker in a culture that was far more risk averse.

Tam sometimes wondered where that risk-taking attitude came from and decided that much of it came from the fact that she had few choices in the beginning of her career and that the rich array of choices that came her way later in America supported risk taking rather than a sense of loss.

Where did Tam go after these failures? She withdrew. She did what she always wanted to do: Teach and write. It was not a decision she "thought through," or weighed or discussed with a mentor. It was a decision driven by instinct, obstinacy, and acceptance of the loneliness inherent in teaching and writing.

Chapter Seven
No More Women

The men in the faculty had an image of women generally and professional women lawyers in particular. As one of the professors explained, women students study hard and are average achievers. "Like Belgium horses," the professors must have thought. "These horses cannot race. Women cannot compete either; they have no intellectual elegance. There is no spark of insight or brilliance in them. But they can drag along."

There was another professor who used to walk in the corridor and announce loudly about one or another person's "second-rate mind." "First-rate minds" were few and certainly not among the women. He was the one who made the statement that Tam heard years later: "We Are Not Going to Hire Any More Women; Look at the Mistake We Have Made with Tam."

When women candidates for faculty were discussed, there were always reservations and even greater reservations about the women candidates who were alumna of the school. These women went to teach in other schools and did quite well. The attitude towards women alumna was similar to that of Groucho Marx who was famous for saying that he would never join or seek membership in a club that accepted him.

Years later, Tam remembered how this colleague met her in the corridor and remarked about an article that she had recently published. The article was not very good. He stopped her and asked: "Why did you write this, Tam? No one will ever read it."

She was not devastated. That was not her nature. But the encounter was not pleasant, either. Then, two days or so later, she received a telephone call from the Chief Justice of a neighboring state. He said: "We are considering an issue similar to the one you discussed in your article, and found no authority except the authority cited in footnote 12 of the article. Do you, by chance, have other authorities on this same point?"

"Do I ever!" said Tam. She hurried to her file cabinet and took out her folders chock full of authorities. She wrote a memo to the Chief Justice who acknowledged it with a copy of the decision citing Tam's article and the footnote.

Tam made a bee line to the Dean with the copy of the decision. She did not contact her critical colleague. The Dean did that.

"But what does this show?" thought Tam. "The article is still not very good, and the cite does not make it better. But the cite did do something. It made the article useful. After all, this is one of the purposes of scholarship. So perhaps if I cannot write great works," thought Tam, "I could write useful works, which other, perhaps greater scholars, or judges, or practitioners might find useful. After all, their use would leave an impact. That is the power that would satisfy me."

"What causes my colleagues to denigrate women?" wondered Tam. "After all, they are happily married, or at least some of them are. They do not seem to hate women. And in Israel there were so many women lawyers, prosecutors, judges, including Supreme Court judges, early on, as well as a prime minister and many powerful women. I think," she mused, "it is because they expect the professional women to behave in the law school context the way their wives behave at home."

Tam concluded that, in America, women had played for some time only one role: the homemaker. Men sometimes play more than one role: that of an employer or employee, a husband and father, a lover or friend. Looking at the way her student women were dressed, she recognized the need for some changes. "How should I instruct them, without telling them?" She thought. "The best way is for me to dress properly, in a suit. Change the blouse but not the suit. Wear jewelry and makeup, but not too much."

Tam soon discovered that women students were concerned about their ability to have a career as well as be married and have children. She began to invite students to her home. There, her three-year-old son, Michael, would bring out a tray of homemade cookies and entice the students: "Try this. It is good. I ate one in the kitchen." Then there was a husband, too, and a large house as well: A home.

Years later, Tam received a letter out of the blue from a person she did not recognize. The writer was a federal court judge, a former prosecutor, and a former senior partner at a large law firm. She was married and had four children. Tam was close to tears because the writer told her that, in law school, she and her friends were concerned about their ability to get married and have children once they embarked on a career. The writer told her that visiting Tam's home made a difference in the women students' belief that it was possible to have a home and a three-year-old and a husband and a legal career as well.

"It is how you view yourself," thought Tam. "It is not how others view you. But if the society as a whole, or those around you, view you as a freak because you have a mind and use it, then it is very difficult to believe that you are not a freak or to continue using your mind. Therefore, in order to overcome this possibility, you must have a critical mass of persons like you. Then, and only then, can you become viewed like others—that is, like the men. Is not that a paradox? To be recognized as a professional woman, a woman must be viewed as a man."

"But when will men truly view women as professionals?" Tam mused. "Maybe when they recognize that women can play different roles, including the role of a professional as well as the role of a lover, a wife and a mother. No words will be effective. Only action and numbers. Would that help?"

Tam remembered that some men were very hostile to professional women, even if the men did not realize how hostile, like the colleague who announced that it was a mistake to hire Tam. There were many like him in those years. What drove him to this attitude? Perhaps the answer was that, if he considered manhood to equate with power, a professional woman represented to him a threat. After all, a man would need not show any virtues to be superior. His sex, and not effort, is what was necessary to place him in this power position. But if a woman becomes a competitor, he might lose the power. Sex would not help him retain it.

In America, unlike in Israel, the assumption is that work done by a woman worthy of praise is mistaken as a man's work even though in reality it was the work of a woman. An example is the following letter:

THE WHITE HOUSE

WASHINGTON

April 24, 1997

Honorable John Kerry
United States Senate
Washington, DC 20510

Dear Senator Kerry:

On behalf of the President, let me thank you for your recent letter of recommendation on behalf of Tamar Frankel. Our administration appreciates your help in identifying quality candidates.

You speak highly of Mr. Frankel's qualifications and I have carefully noted your insights and support. I have shared your letter with the appropriate staff and would like you to know that your comments will receive full consideration.

On behalf of President Clinton, we welcome your views and hope that we can count on your continued support.

Sincerely,

Bob J. Nash
Assistant to the President and
Director of Presidential Personnel

cc: Mr. Tamar Frankel
20 Pleasantview Terrace
Framingham, MA 01701

White House personnel twice ignored the female name "Tamar" to refer to Tam as a man, Mr. Tamar Frankel. Finally, the position of women in America is changing so that it is not always assumed that anyone receiving an honor is likely to be a man, not a woman.

Tam did not spend much time or thought on these issues. She continued to do "her thing." During the first year of her career at the law school, she was assigned space in the basement of the library instead of an office. That delighted her. She could keep the books she was using and did not have to return them to the shelf. That was a privilege. The students found her wherever she was, and colleagues could find her if they wanted to talk to her. In that place, she wrote her S.J.D. thesis on variable annuities.

These small triumphs sustained Tam. But they did not deceive her. She knew she was lacking. She tried hard never to read anything that she published. It was too painful to discover the blemishes, the undeveloped ideas, and the absence of perfection. Perfection is what she strove for, knowing pretty well that she would not achieve it. But no other criterion was satisfactory. It took years before she could forgive herself for imperfect work. Forgive, yes. But never deceive herself that she reached perfection. Besides, what would she do when she reached the stage, if at all possible? It comforted her that perfection was not possible. Thank God for that.

Chapter Eight
Loneliness

Tam's appointment to the faculty did not run as smoothly as she imagined. In part, her imagination was based on lack of information about what was happening within the school's faculty. In part, her imagination was based on total lack of understanding of the system. And in part, she was not interested in the system, so long as it allowed her to do the two things she wanted: teach and write. When she met the Dean to discuss her possible appointment, she was asked what were her salary conditions. Tam was surprised. In Israel at that time, a new employee was paid a fixed amount depending on seniority. So the starting salary was the same for everyone starting at that level. It did not occur to her that she could or should bargain for a salary. She answered faintly: "Whatever is a fair amount." And let it be at that.

The Dean nodded and that ended the conversation on this item. Tam also did not understand the meaning and importance of tenure. Job security was quite strong in Israel. People were not easily fired unless there was a very good reason. Besides, she did not particularly care. If this job was not available, there would be others, she was sure. She had no idea how much she needed a mentor. So she agreed to a three-year contract and started teaching at Boston University.

During the three years, some colleagues appeared in her classroom from time to time. One in particular was obvious by his behavior. The students noted him listening carefully and furiously writing in his notebook. Tam did not particularly care that he listened or wrote, and that was a blessing. But the

33

students, and especially the women students, were more savvy. They noticed the nodding and frowning and repeated class visits. It was the students who went to the Dean and demanded that Tam be given tenure. Ignorance can be a blessing. The pressures and jostling and disagreements passed by Tam. She just taught and wrote. Then one day, the Dean called to tell her that the faculty recommended her for a tenure position and a colleague passed her in the corridor, hugged her and congratulated her on the great news.

Years later, Tam thought: "I was such an idiot. I did not understand nor was I interested in finding out how important tenure was. Instead, I wondered over the big focus on it. Was I that stupid? Yes, I was. But how lucky too! Perhaps I am stupid today as well. I might be a bit more aware of the culture and people's assumptions and expectations and difficulties. But I was not caught up by all this. I was free, though stupendously ignorant. I remained free. But I paid the price."

The price was loneliness. There was loneliness at work. There was loneliness even as one went to dinner parties and gave dinner parties. One felt the strangeness of others and one's own. Tam used to listen to the conversation and wonder: "Everyone agrees with everyone else. Most topics are mundane, including the weather, or the children, what they said and how they said it. The child said: "Oh, Mom. Look at the red balloon? Does it not look like a red Mommy's dress." And people would burst into peals of laughter.

Arguments were not acceptable. Everyone pretty much agreed with everything. In contrast, Tam remembered dinner parties in Israel. We would bring flowers or chocolate or a bottle of wine and sit on the veranda or in the dining room. Then the conversation would often turn to issues of politics. Mr. Peres, for example, was always on the labor party's side and one of the guests would always be on the minority party's side, and others simply had their own opinions, regardless of the parties' positions.

At one dinner party hosted by Mr. Peres, Tam remembered the arguments on whether the Gaza Strip should continue to be occupied or let go. The Army people at the table argued for continued occupation. It would be safer, they insisted. The Gaza Strip would serve as a barrier against the Egyptians who had attacked Israel time and again and reached too close to the Jewish town of Beersheba before they were driven back. Others at the table argued that Israel should never have second-class citizens. No democracy can survive if it treats some segment of its population differently. And yet, how could the residents of the Gaza Strip be recruited into the Army or given other positions requiring loyalty to Israel? It is difficult enough that the West Bank Arab residents do not serve in the Army. At least they can be compared to the religious Jews that are exempt from serving. But here are many more Arabs, and how can they be integrated into the Jewish state?

That evening, like many others, people got excited, sometimes banged on the table, and raised their voices. When the time came to depart, everyone would hug everyone else and declare: "This was a wonderful evening!" Tam would never forget that specific evening because everyone cared so much. The heated arguing brought everyone in the group together rather than separating them. They shared the deep caring they felt for the country. Besides, arguing is a Jewish trait with which everyone is comfortable.

"What an evening!" she thought longingly. "But who knows: Israelis may behave differently today at a dinner party. So stop thinking longingly for what has past. And what is so good about the culture of a debating society instead of a culture that brings a consensus? OK. When danger is prominent or imminent, the arguments stop. But only until the danger is over. Oh, time to go to sleep. And besides, there is a class to prepare tomorrow early in the morning."

Chapter Nine
The Different Way of Speaking

Accent can be deeply ingrained. Tam had a student who could not pronounce the letter "L" and spoke of the duty of "Royalty" instead of the duty of "Loyalty" in corporate law. The student went so far as to write a paper in which the duty of Loyalty was spelled the duty of Royalty. His accent dictated the spelling as well.

Tam worried about her own accent. What can a teacher do if she has a foreign accent? What can a teacher do when she has students who speak with different accents? She decided to seek the advice of an expert in phonetics and found one at M.I.T. He was kind enough to meet with her. She also read about the subject.

"What is the secret of speaking without an accent?" she asked.

"You should not speak without an accent" he replied. "An accent can be an asset. But it should be modulated. If the accent is slight, and the students have to strain their ears just a bit to follow, that raises their attention. That is good. If the accent is too heavy and the strain is too great, the students would turn off and cease to try and follow. You already have an accent. Keep it. Besides, you cannot completely eradicate it. Let us learn how to make it slighter."

Tam learned a number of techniques to clarify her pronunciation. Mostly, she learned to make sure that she clearly pronounced the last letter in the word.

"No swallowing of a letter is ever allowed," said the teacher. "Like the word allowed. The "d" is the key to clear pronunciation of the word allowed. And if you can guess last or first letter that the students swallow in their pronunciation, you might understand them better, too."

It was like magic. Students understood Tam better and she understood them better. The teacher, who was a clever psychiatrist, also gave good advice on structuring the class.

"Imagine," he said, "structuring the class as a train, the first part driving each part, and building on it. Or you can start from the core idea and expand it by wide and wider circles."

Chapter Ten
Legal Education for the British Colonies

The Jerusalem Law Classes in which Tam learned law was a peculiar law school designed by the British for the colonies. It seems that lawyers were not on the list of favored occupations for the natives. Besides, the Jewish population was not the most favored by the British authorities. The Jews were too clever, too educated, not very servile, and arrogant. The Civil Service in the colonies was not the choice civil service position. The British Chief Justice in Palestine during the period of the mandatory reign returned to England to become a judge in the land court (a less prestigious court). The wealthy Arab landowners in Palestine were far more amiable, less educated, wealthier, and easier to deal with.

The relationship between the students and teachers in the Jerusalem Law Classes reflected the view of the British authorities of the population and the policies underlying the education of lawyers for the colonies. To cut down the number of lawyers, the five-year program consisted of three stages. In a two-year first stage, the students first listened to lectures. There were no seminars nor any interaction with the teachers. At the end of the two years, students took twelve three-hour exams, one a day for four days each week over three weeks. Failure of a single exam required a student to retake the two-year course and repeat the exams.

One student, a public official, probably age 35 when Tam knew him, was a permanent student for many years. He was known to explain: "I know all the answers and I know all the questions. But I do not know which answer to put to each question."

Memory was the key to passing these exams. One was expected to know the names of both parties and the facts. It was then fairly easy to use the cases to answer the questions. The questions followed pretty much the notes of the lectures.

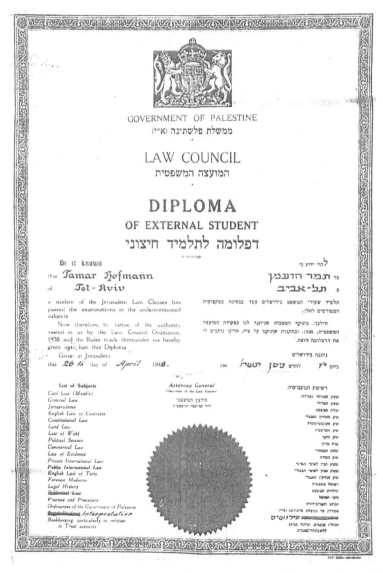

Diploma from the Government of Palestine, Law Council for completion of the Jerusalem Law Classes.

The second two years followed the same pattern as the first two years, but the number of exams dropped to eight and the duration of the exams to two weeks. Then came the last year, ending with five exams. Again, rote memorization was the key to success. Thereafter, students were required to spend two years as apprentices in a lawyer's office and, upon completion of this clerkship, they could receive their diploma. Thus, the normal process for law school required five years of lectures and exams, followed by two apprentice years. If they had reached the age of 23, the students with a diploma could receive a certificate allowing them to practice law.

However, students were allowed to be absentee students for the last two years of lectures if they became apprentices during that time. The enormous burden on students' memory could be relieved somewhat if the student developed some analytical skills. To be sure, learning the names, facts and outcomes without a conceptual structure rendered the development of analytical skills difficult.

Tam studied hard for the first two years and passed all exams. The next two years were easier and the last one, she spent clerking for her father. That year she learned a lot. He was a good teacher. But even before that time, he taught her and she worked in the office, she became a reporter in the arbitration proceedings that he conducted and discussed law with him. That helped her organize the materials in her mind and pass the exams.

After the years of classes and exams and her apprenticeship, Tam was granted the very first license to practice law in Israel in April 1949.

ISRAEL WOMAN LAWYER

TEL AVIV, Israel (WNS)—The first license to practice law in Isreal was given to a woman in uniform, Flight Lieutenant Tamar Werber of the Israeli Air Force, daughter of the Chairman of the Israel Bar Association, Mr. A Hoffman. Her husband, Major Yehuda Werber, and pilot officer Shmuel Reiter, were also among the seven advocates to be admitted to the bar by a modest ceremony, the first of its kind, at which Mr. Justice Smoira, President of the Supreme Court, took the call.

B'nai B'rith Messenger, 8 April 1949. Historical Jewish Press, The National Library of Israel and Tel Aviv University.

Chapter Eleven
The Profession as a Home/Loss of Privacy

Dushinka came from Russia and married Max, German born. They had a very good marriage and both played poker very well. Especially Dushinka. She did not work outside the home and had much time on her hands to find out about the neighbors. But she was a giving good soul. They, as well as Tam and her husband, lived in a housing community group established for Army officers; all of them knew each other well.

On one occasion when Tam and Dushinka met, she asked Tam: "Why do you eat so much pudding?"

Tam responded: "Dushinka! How do you know how much pudding we eat?"

Dushinka answered without hesitation and with a bit of surprise: "I looked in your refrigerator."

Tam accepted the price of intrusion and viewed it as "normal." The other aspect of the same behavior, however, was compensatory. Dushinka was a true friend. Tam knew that if she ever needed help—any help—Dushinka would not hesitate for a moment to help as much as she could.

As this incident reflects, the feeling of security brought about by the culture of involvement has a price. In an environment of danger, the price is not considered high. Yet, it was recognized. The price is loss of privacy to a greater or lesser degree. When everyone involved is implicitly agreeing to protect you, then your private affairs become everyone's business.

A group intrusion on people's behavior is not always welcome. The group may set different standards of behavior and impose those standards on individuals engaged in what they believe to be private business. One example included a mother-son relationship. Years ago, a mother gave her son, about ten or twelve years old, a good thrashing in the middle of the street. Where she came from and given her son's prior behavior, she believed it was an acceptable thing to do. But in Tel Aviv, passersby believed it was far too harsh. For a few minutes, passersby stood and watched. As the beating did not stop, a number of spectators formed a group around the woman and the child, and one, or a few, directed the mother in no uncertain terms to stop! It was quite obvious that, if she did not stop, they would make her stop.

She sniffed, said that it was none of the spectators' business, but discontinued beating and led the child away.

One of the spectators called after her: "We do not do this here. Remember!"

Chapter Twelve
Hatred of Brothers

There is a saying that Jerusalem—the capital of the Jewish State centuries ago—fell not because it was conquered by the Romans, but because of the "hatred of brothers." This is a translation that may not give the full flavor of the meaning in Hebrew.

Tam was a member of a high school class. A third of her class members died fighting for the establishment of a State of Israel. Another third was in the Haganah and many of these were later in the Israeli military or members of the legal division in the new government.

Tam remembers Haim Cohen, General Director of the Ministry of Justice, her superior at the legal division (later a Supreme Court judge), ordering the arrest of the religious Jews who threw stones at a bus that was in service on Saturday.

Tam also remembers the murder of the beloved Prime Minister by a religious Jew. Jews have carried the curse of fighting among themselves. They are the worst enemies of their own Jewish nation. It is not surprising that Prime Minister Ben Gurion refused to mention religion in the statement of Israel's establishment.

David Ben Gurion took a rigid, uncompromising position: There will be only one Army in Israel. No other armed groups will be allowed nor recognized, but the leadership of the two other groups that sought to form armies would have a political place in the government and the legislature. This solution retained the other two groups' power.

Chapter Thirteen
Holocaust Memories

Born in or come to Israel before it became an independent state, the Israelis violated the British rulers and stealthily at night brought the remnants of the Holocaust by ships and "spread" them in various settlements. Some of these people found their homes in Settlements, and some in pre-built small two- or three-room apartments that were connected to each others' walls because land was easier to have than building high-level building and also easier to share.

For a first-born in Israel, as Tam was, the new arrivals were very different.

First, they had numbers etched on their lower arms.

Second, they ate by holding their plates with their arms around them. And when they were told: "You need not hold to your plate, no one will take it from you." The answer was an apologetic: "Yes, I know, but it is more convenient for me to hold it this way." An Israeli's blood pressure, who heard such an answer, would rise significantly on hearing such an answer, and his and her teeth would grit. How could anyone give up his or her freedom?

Abba Kovener, a remnant and leader of another group of Jews in Poland, had an explanation for how many Jews gave up their freedom and what he described is the process of the Jews who ended in the extermination camps. The extermination camps were not the beginning and the end, but just the end of the Jews who perished there in a horrible manner.

It started with a first step: (1) You may not have a telephone.
— Reaction: This is not so bad.

Then (2) You may not walk on the pavement but only on the street with the horse-carriages. — Reaction: This is not so bad either.

Then (3) You must wear a yellow sign on the front of your dress and jacket. — Reaction: one can live with this too.

Then (4) You must go on the train. — Reaction: Okay, it is better than walking.

(5) The trip ends in the extermination camp.

What we learned from these stories: One should never give an inch of one's personal freedom and due honor. As an Israeli, this lesson was engraved in my soul.

This discussion may seem to have moved away from the Holocaust, but in fact it did not.

If the discrimination of Jews is moving towards physical danger, it is time to move out to a safer place. It may be a prison but a safe one. That is what Israel was established to provide: a safer place and it actually does so. It is a model.

No country around the world and even on the moon or other planets may establish an extermination camp for Jews who are too weak to reject the deadly frustration of others. Attempts have been are made, but the world is reacting rather than accepting and nips such behavior in the bud.

Chapter Fourteen
Elie Wiesel Introduction[*]

Ladies and Gentlemen:

It is a special honor to introduce to you Professor Elie Wiesel. Only a great artist could turn a boyhood horror into the voice of those who suffered the horror. Only a great writer could reach the hearts and minds of those who did not know that such events were at all possible. But it is the truly greatest person who could experience horror, speak about it, and then explain and reach for humanity through inhumanity.

How could the Nazis do such monstrous things to others? Did they lose their own humanity altogether? I suspect that in their eyes they considered themselves human. But in order to be able to torture their victims, they must have considered the victims less human. The Nazis, I believe, did not invent racism merely to feel superior. They needed to create their racial theory in order to justify the atrocities towards Jews and others. Otherwise the Nazis would have found it much harder or perhaps impossible to do what they did.

There is a word, which provides a powerful expression to our relationship with each other and to society as a whole. This word is identity. Identity has three meanings. They conflict with each other, and complement each other.

"Identity" implies separateness. Each of us has his or hers own identity that distinguishes us from each other. But the word "identical," emanating from the same root means precisely the opposite. It describes things that are one and the same, and

* Tam's Introduction to the Lecture given by Nobel Prize Holder Elie Wiesel on Anti-Semitism, November 10, 2003.

49

impossible to distinguish. We are not identical. We are different from each other.

In addition to feeling identical we have the word to "identify." It does not mean sameness. It means, among other meanings, to "recognize" and "associate." It means the capacity to imagine how others feel, even though the others are different from us, and separate from us. Thus, each person has his or her own identity, but most persons can identify with others.

How can that be? How can we imagine what others feel, even though we are separate and different from them? The answer is that identity is complex and consists of many features. We can identify with each other because we share one feature of our identity in common. We share our humanity. Regardless of how we look, act, feel, and behave, we are all human. If we share our humanity, we are able to identify with other humans.

The ability to identify with others is fundamental to our nature as individuals and to society. Identifying with others is important to our emotional well-being because we cannot tolerate total aloneness. This deep feeling is necessary to our survival. Total separation endangers our survival.

But the ability to identify with others is as crucial to the existence of civil society. This ability to identify protects us from each other. Once we identify with others, we hurt ourselves when we harm others. But if we do not identify, we can hurt others with impunity. Thus, to hurt others we must sever the bond—the feature of identity that is common to all. We must render the others non-human, and view them as animals or even as things.

This brings me to Professor Wiesel's topic of this evening's lecture: Anti-Semitism, in the Past and Today. I speculate again, that anti-Semitism is a way in which people dehumanize others.

Very few people sever the bond of humanity in its entirety and consider all others to be non-human. But some can sever their bond of humanity with particular groups. Anti-Semites sever their bonds with a select group of humans and thereby minimize and shrink their own ability to bond themselves to humanity. Not their victims, but they become less human.

Therefore, anti-Semitism does not hurt only, and perhaps not mainly, Jews. Often Jews can protect themselves from hatred and its dangers. We have survived thousands of years under its pressure. Anti-Semitism corrupts those who practice it. It corrodes their spirit. It shrinks their world, and isolates them. While in their mind they reduce the humanity of others, they thereby reduce their own.

Chapter Fifteen
Experiences as a Visiting Scholar and the Like

Some years passed writing and teaching as a faculty member at Boston University Law School, and Tam began to receive invitations to be a visiting scholar, to teach for a semester or more at another law school and to speak at various occasions. She accepted the invitations that fit into her schedule and offered her exposure and the opportunity to learn.

1979-1980: Visiting Professor of Law, Harvard Law School

Fall 1980: Visiting Professor of Business Management, Harvard Business School

1982-1983: Visiting Professor of Law, University of California Law School, Berkeley, California

April-June 1997: Visiting Professor, Graduate School of Law and Politics, University of Tokyo, Japan, where she lectured, among other things, on Trust and Contract in the U.S. and Japan, with Norio Higuchi

Oct.-Dec. 2000: Visiting Fellow, St. Catherine's College; Center for Social-Legal Studies and Wolfson College, Oxford University, Oxford England

Sept.-June 2005: Visiting Professor, Harvard Law School

Jan.-June 2006: Visiting Professor, Harvard Business School

In addition, Tam was a Faculty Fellow at the Berkman Klein Center for Internet and Society, a research center at Harvard University, as well serving as an advisor on the American Law Institute Restatement of the Law (Third) of Trusts (Prudent

Investors Rule). She testified before Congress concerning banking and securities law reform.

Tam accepted offers to serve as a guest scholar or attorney fellow at private or government institutions at the heart of the federal government. Most notably, she was twice an attorney fellow at the SEC, learning and offering her advice directly to personnel at the Commission after having praised and criticized their work in her four-volume work, *The Regulation of Money Managers*, and in numerous articles.

Jan-1986-Aug. 1987: Guest Scholar, The Brookings Institution Washington, D.C.

July-Dec. 1995: Attorney Fellow, Securities and Exchange Commission, Washington, D.C.

July 1996-July 1997: Attorney Fellow, Securities and Exchange Commission, Washington, D.C.

Tam was asked to speak to organizations and groups on multiple occasions. She spoke to a group at Mitsubishi Bank in Japan in 1998, explaining the importance of following fiduciary principles even in a world in which some competitors did not do so. As she explained, translated from Japanese:

> Mitsubishi members practice fiduciary behavior and duties. They can show that these duties are not only burdensome, but that over time, they are also profitable and satisfying. As a life-long teacher I can assure you that there is great satisfaction in showing and leading people to act honestly.

In 2006, Tam spoke at IDC Herzliya Radzyner School of Law in Israel on the "Fall of the Barriers Preventing Abuse of Trust and Deception: The Hidden Changes in Legal Doctrine and Legal Interpretation."

Tam accepted the invitation to give the University Lecture at Boston University on October 10, 2012. Once a year, a professor or other individual is invited to give this lecture, and she took the invitation as a sign she was finally accepted after all the years being on the outside or the margins of the University. Her lecture was entitled "The Ponzi Scheme Puzzle: A History and Analysis of Con Artists and Victims," and drew on the book of the same name she had published that year.

In November 2019, Tam spoke to Harvard Hillel on the concepts addressed in her book *Living in Different Cultures*. She described that book as "the Bar Mitzva of my books—the 12th book," dealing with the personal experiences of an Israeli woman living in different cultures.

She consulted with the People's Bank of China and lectured in Canada, Geneva, India, Kuala Lumpur, Malaysia, and Switzerland. Tam was also the advisor for a visiting scholar from Egypt who was studying at Boston University Law School (2020-2021). Some of the work they did included writing on the topic of "Legal Education for Lawyers."

Chapter Sixteen
Working Together Is Better

In the 1990s, Tam was asked to provide advice for setting up a not-for-profit organization in Virginia. Sure, she said, agreeing. It was only later that Tam learned the unique nature of this not-for-profit corporation. It was designed to hold the key to the Internet that had been developed by the United States Army.

As businesses first learned of the possibilities the Internet promised, business organizations claimed the right to participate not only in its use, but also in its control.

The "techies" and the business parties argued before Congress and lobbied the White House, but could not come to agreement. The White House recommended that the parties meet in Virginia in another attempt to come to an agreement. Tam was asked to help identify a structure and naming terminology that all the interested parties could accept.

Needless to say, Tam knew nothing about the Internet, but she did know something about corporate law, which she was teaching. Before the meeting, the experts tutored her about the Internet and the organization as it existed. Tam received a stunning number of e-mails, some demanding time at the meeting to present their views.

It became clear that the past procedures and practices would not bear fruit. When Tam arrived at the hotel in Virginia, she asked for a number of changes. First, news   reporters were not to be allowed into the meeting. Second, the hall in which the members of all parties were to meet would be divided into five spaces and each space would have a blackboard. The meeting participants numbered about 500 persons.

Instead of individual presentations, Tam proposed that the process should follow these rules: The five blackboard stations each held part of the design of the corporation that the participants were about to create. Participants were encouraged to move from station to station and argue to their hearts' content. However, by evening that day, each group must report on any agreement reached concerning the items noted in the stations: (i) the name of the organization, (ii) the number of the directors, (iii) the position of International Countries and (iv) a few other such items. They should report only what they agreed upon. And they should determine who would report the results.

At the end of the day, each group came forward and its representative proudly presented its decision, the name, the structure and other details were generally but clearly established. There was a feeling of "high" in the audience, a feeling of achievement, achievement of something great and productive. It was a "winning" but a different kind of winning.

Competitors, especially if their expertise complements each other, may find that working together is better for both: not arguing and rejecting but instead agreeing. The agreement may be more rewarding than standing rigidly on a position.

Later, Tam traveled to Switzerland and Singapore and spoke to a group in South America. The interested parties adopted the structure, and the Internet Corporation for Assigned Names and Numbers (ICANN) was born.

As Tam had hoped, when people had the opportunity to build together something great, new, and ambitious, they found far more satisfaction than in winning against each other. That "something new" became the Internet.

On International Women's Day in 2022, ICANN celebrated Tam as "an inspiring woman who played a key role in the formation of ICANN and the creation of the multistakeholder model."[*]

---

[*]   See https://www.icann.org/en/blogs/details/celebrating-an-important-woman-in-icanns-history-07-03-2022-en.

Chapter Seventeen
Prizes and Awards

In 2013, the Institute for Fiduciary Standard established the annual Frankel Fiduciary Prize in her honor to award individuals who advance fiduciary principles. Commodity Futures Trading Commission Chairman Brooksley Born (1996-99) remarked at the time, December 9, 2013, that no one embodies fiduciary principles better than Tam. "She has been teaching and writing and speaking and researching on fiduciary law, regulation, ethics and behavior since I met her 48 years ago." Tam "befriended me and offered guidance." She added:

> Her books include definitive texts on fiduciary law, regulation of investment managers and investment advisers, and most recently, a timely analyses of Ponzi schemes, perhaps the ultimate in investor fraud as demonstrated by Mr. Madoff. She has played an enormous role in articulating the importance of strengthening and extending the fiduciary standard to a broad range of investment managers and advisers, ranging from broker dealers to corporate directors.

On the occasion of its 150th Anniversary, Boston University School of Law recognized Tam as the "godmother of the fiduciary rule" and recognized the creation of the Frankel Fiduciary Prize "to acknowledge individuals who have made significant contributions to the preservation and advancement of fiduciary principles in public life." The annual awarding of the Prize has become an opportunity for a symposium.

Mitsubishi Bank created a Museum of Trust in Tokyo and in other countries and invited Tam to open the Museum with the chairman of Mitsubishi Bank. Tam recognized the Museum as "an example of a long-term effort to reduce the cost of mistrust and breach of trust" and observed that "American banks and other institutions, such as schools, can create similar educational museums of their own in the US and add to the history of trust and to an explanation of its crucial role in America's economy and culture." Tam's book, *Fiduciary Law* (Oxford University Press; 1st edition, Dec. 17, 2010), was translated into Japanese and given to leaders of the bank, visiting lawyers, and others at the museum opening.

In January 2018, Tam received the Ruth Bader Ginsburg Lifetime Achievement Award. The purpose of this Award is to honor an individual who has had a distinguished career of teaching, service, and scholarship over at least 20 years. The recipient should be someone who has impacted women, the legal community, and the issues that affect women through mentoring, writing, speaking, activism, and by providing opportunities to others.

Tam was noted as one of 500 lawyers who have made a remarkable contribution to the profession as an innovator and are named to Lawdragon's Hall of Fame in 2015 and as one of the Women Trailblazers in the Law by the ABA Commission on Women in the Profession in 2007. Her oral history was taken over multiple days in 2007-08, as part of a collaborative research project between the American Bar Association and the American Bar Foundation. Finally, Wealth Manager Web named Tam among the 50 Top Women in Wealth Management in 2010. In February 2021, she created The Investors First Podcast hosted by Chris Cannon, CFA, Chief Investment Officer at FirsTrust and board member for CFA Society of Orlando and explaining why she spent her career focusing on fiduciary law and what it means to be a fiduciary, conflicts of interest within the advisory world and her regulatory suggestions to help eliminate them.

Chapter Eighteen
Retirement and Experiences in Later Years

Tam retired June 30, 2018 at the age of 92. Shortly after retirement, Tam was awarded emerita status, and the Law School Dean Angela Onwuachi-Willig responded with a kind and thoughtful letter recognizing the work Tam had done over the years and her many contributions to the Law School.

Boston University School of Law

765 Commonwealth Avenue
Boston, Massachusetts 02215
T 617-353-3112 F 617-358-4706

Angela Onwuachi-Willig
Dean and Professor of Law

March 2, 2021

VIA E-MAIL

Re: Emeritus Status at Boston University

Dear Tamar,

It is my great pleasure to inform you that, by a unanimous vote of the law faculty, I am authorized to designate you Emerita Professor of Law. Although this vote occurred previously, we recently learned that you may not have been notified of your emeritus status. If so, we wanted to be sure to provide you with a formal recognition of this honor. With this letter, I am proud to designate you Emerita Professor of Law. As you know, Emerita is a status of honor and esteem at Boston University that is intended to recognize professors for lifetime contributions to the University, to their field, or to both, upon their retirement.

In granting your Emerita status, the faculty took note of the following facts: You received your diploma from the Jerusalem Law Classes in 1948, the same year that the State of Israel came into existence. Your graduation from law school was the start of a journey to which the word "remarkable" does not do justice.

After serving terms as Assistant Legal Advisor in the Israeli Air Force and Assistant Attorney General in Israel's Ministry of Justice and spending more than a decade as a private lawyer in Israel, you arrived in Boston in 1963 to get an LL.M. from Harvard Law School. We seldom find nice things to say about Harvard in this part of town, but all hail Harvard's 1963 LL.M. program for bringing Professor Tamar Frankel to the United States! After stops at Ropes & Gray, Arnold & Porter, and the California Commissioner of Corporations, you graced Boston University School of Law by becoming a Lecturer at the school in 1967. The following year, in 1968, you joined the faculty as an Assistant Professor of Law, and as the first female professor in the law school's history. That momentous hiring was commemorated by giving you an office in the basement of the school's law library, which did not dampen the fire in your spirit one bit. Indeed, I hear you secretly relished your basement office because it enabled you to write your highly impactful scholarship without interruption. And, wow! What a trail you blazed with your groundbreaking research! You also blazed a trail that opened doors for all the women faculty who have followed you, including me. Thank you!

More than fifty years later, nobody puts "the Tamar Frankel" in a basement. After half a century of teaching, writing, advising, probing, questioning, and inspiring, you are a worldwide force of nature. You have authored ten books and dozens of articles, many of which are classics in the fields of corporate, financial, and fiduciary law. It is not quite adequate to say that you wrote the book – actually, two books – on securitization; you essentially invented the field. Your work on fiduciary law and theory has influenced scholars, lawmakers, regulators, and financial giants across the globe. The Institute for the Fiduciary Standard named its annual prize, given "to a person who has made significant contributions to the preservation and advancement of fiduciary principles in public life," http://www.thefiduciaryinstitute.org/the-frankel-fiduciary-prize/, the Frankel Fiduciary Prize. The AALS Section on Women in Legal Education gave you the Ruth Bader Ginsburg Lifetime Achievement Award, which is designed "to honor an individual who has had a distinguished career of teaching, service, and scholarship for at least 20 years . . . [and] has impacted women, the legal community, the academy, and the issues that affect women through mentoring, writing, speaking, activism, and by providing opportunities to others." You were also named the Robert B. Kent Professor at Boston University School of Law. This litany could go on for quite some time.

All of these accomplishments, along with numerous others and several thousand Google scholar citations, do not begin to communicate your contributions to the law school, the legal profession, and our society. You have been an outstanding teacher, an exemplary colleague, and a truly unique role model. Even in retirement, you continue to produce scholarship, and you have continue to influence and inspire all of us in the coming years. For all of these reasons, and many more, I am delighted to formally grant you the title Professor Emerita of Law. Congratulations! We look forward to your continuing affiliation with our scholarly community.

Warmest Regards,

Angela Onwuachi-Willig
Dean and Professor of Law

Boston University celebrated the Law School's 150 years of operation in 2023, printing a handsome, quite large book including many of the professors who taught during part of those years and included Tam. The book is helpful for refreshing Tam's memory of the many colleagues she worked with over the years.

From time to time, Tam receives communications from people she has known for a long time, former colleagues, people she has met traveling and others. They correspond by letters, emails, and meetings with her on occasion. Tam appreciates keeping in contact with her professional friends and people with whom she was connected before. Other than the COVID years, she enjoys meeting them in her house, their house or outside the house. Although years may pass, the connection remains, often very strong.

In addition, Tam has participated in a mentoring group that connects seniors with college students. The college students learn how world used to be, and the seniors catch up with some of the many changes. These mentoring sessions occur September through June, when the students are in their college living arrangements. Tam has had three college students so far. Students are required to write up what they got out of the mentoring meetings with Tam, and the students appear to be as enthusiastic as Tam is.

Since retirement, Tam has primarily engaged in writing. In addition to her book, *Living in Different Cultures*, she has written articles published in Verdict—Legal Analysis and Commentary, Advisor Perspectives, American Bar Association, Business Law Section, and elsewhere.

Tam began writing on the topic of "Aging" after retirement, and this subject remains in process. Although much of Tam's thinking on aging is not ready to share widely, she is pleased to provide the following excerpt of her thoughts.

We age from the day we are born. Our worlds typically expand from just family to school classmates, to friends and later colleagues at work. With retirement, however, our worlds may shrink, as our social, study, as well as workworlds diminish: friends, family members and colleagues die or move away. Our worlds may also shrink because we may have experienced physical or cognitive losses over time, making it difficult to do certain activities or making us lack the energy to participate in outside activities. Because our outside worlds influence our inner world, when we have major losses, our minds may be affected by experiencing pervasive sadness or depression, especially when some or all of the losses may not be replaceable.

To be sure, it is possible to create a rich life despite physical and mental infirmity, although different from the one we had before. This possibility may become a reality depending on our resilience, our ability to understand and adjust to loss, and whether we can sense and adapt to opportunities to find other sources of fulfillment.

The challenge posed by aging is whether we can enrich and re-build a fulfilling, more independent, inner life despite external and internal losses. We need to build and maintain a fulfilling inner life, that then drives our external life. It can be done in many ways: such as reading, writing, thinking, listening to lectures and music, talking with friends, making new friends, or teaching and learning something new or reliving positive experiences and learning new areas of knowledge. These are all life-affirming activities that offer new pleasure, reduce emptiness and darkness, and open the door to light. One can learn and develop one's abilities by living or interacting in places and with people of other cultures and new interests. An individual that matures, then ages, can develop emotionally and create a rich and fulfilling inner landscape despite impairments. Sadly, not all do.

There is a somewhat indirect lesson to learn from the following story. An old Cherokee spoke with his son:

> My son, visualize a battle between two wolves inside us all. One is Evil. It is anger, envy, jealousy, sorrow, regret, greed, arrogance, self-pity, guilt, resentment, inferiority, lies, false pride, superiority, and ego. The other is Good. It is joy, peace, love, hope, serenity, humility, kindness, benevolence, empathy, generosity, truth, compassion and faith.
>
> The son thought for a minute, then asked his father: "Which wolf wins?"
>
> The old Cherokee replied: "The one you feed."

With age and more time, and perhaps more money than before, a person may be increasingly exposed to the two wolves. An aging person may choose the evil world, to relive internal anger and anguish that person feels and felt earlier in life, or the person may choose the good world to share joy and happiness with others.

Whether free time and perhaps more money that may come with age lead a person to choose the evil world or the good one may be influenced by the lifetime of experiences that went before. Some observe that people become more like themselves as they age. But it comes to a choice each day, sometimes each minute. It depends on each of us and the one we feed.

About the Author

Tamar Frankel was born on July 4, 1925 and raised in the land that later became Israel. She served in the Haganah, a branch of the Israeli underground, before Israel became a State in 1948, and in the Israeli Air Force in its early years. She received a diploma from the Government of Palestine, Law Council for completion of the Jerusalem Law Classes and was issued the first license to practice law in Israel in 1949.

She came to America first in 1949 with a group of Israeli military tasked to speak to Jewish communities about the Israeli War of Independence. In 1963, she was invited to be a visiting scholar at Harvard Law School. She attended Harvard Law School graduating with LL.M. and SJ.D. and became of Professor of Law at Boston University in 1969. Frankel retired in 2018. She specialized in mutual funds, securitization, financial system regulation, fiduciary law and corporate governance. She taught as a visiting scholar at Harvard, University of California Berkeley, Japan and England along with her teaching duties at Boston University.

She was the author of *The Regulation of Money Managers* (1978), now in third edition, as well as *The Ponzi Scheme Puzzle: A History and Analysis of Con Artists and Victims* (2012), *Variable Annuities, Variable Insurance and Separate Accounts* (1971). She completed *Living in Different Cultures*, a form of memoir, in 2019. Following her retirement, she has contributed articles to Verdict-Legal Analysis and Commentary and many other publications.

In 2017, she received the Ruth Bader Ginsburg Lifetime Achievement Award. In 2022, ICANN celebrated Frankel as "an inspiring woman who played a key role in the formation of ICANN."

Printed in the USA
CPSIA information can be obtained
at www.ICGtesting.com
JSHW011133090724
66074JS00006B/17